Weeping
Gang

Bliss Void

Yab-Yum

•

Poems by

Devendra

Banhart

WEEPING GANG
BLISS VOID YAB-YUM

·

POEMS BY
DEVENDRA BANHART

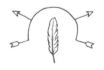

featherproof BOOKS

Published by featherproof Books

First edition
10 9 8 7 6 5 4 3 2 1

Library of Congress Control Number: 2018968072
ISBN 13: 978-1-943888-18-4

Edited by Tim Kinsella
Proofread by Sam Axelrod
Cover Art by Devendra Banhart
Design by Zach Dodson
Portrait by Moses Berkson

Set in Baskerville

All true paths
state it's not
in the adding
on, but the
       peeling away.

The blue sky is turtle
carcass.

One
I want to give
you.

Blue
of the night sky
blue,

Brief
stay, brief
stay.

Petal falls soon
as it appears. Alive
as water, speaking
love's
       firefly language.

Human
night, brief
stay, brief
stay.

Soon, all gone.

It's good luck to kill innumerable innocent people
and drive all manner of creature to extinction.

Once the earthquakes began, they never stopped.
& All else was just a 1000-year-old

Veggie
patty.

End of Sentence

I'm filling up with

No tears.

Asleep atop
the great storm.

Eat the heart of summer.

Sky-resemblance blues.

My head is
my ass.

Moon,
a grave well-earned,
and a cheap wedding
ring.

I forgot
to ask, what was that
song your father
used to sing?

The black snake in my belly is

Home Free.

All the way
home.

Sweet honeyed

Home.

In the deepest
      depths of the loneliest
coal mine,
all that
was found was
kept, catch
my drift?

I am dead.

The wind carries me with it.

This is how
I breathe now.

The wind carries me with it,
wherever
it may

Now
go.

Late last night
snow fell.

& After all
the guests had gone home,
I took a walk

Wearing one of the sweaters you left behind,
wondering if you can feel it
when I wear it.

On   a long   walk,
            a longing walk,
hoping   more & more
to want   less and less.

Hoping to
reappear somewhere far from here,

A thunder cloud
inside a spider's mouth.

Every single day
of my life
I pray,
and at the end
of my prayer

I bow and blow
a kiss to the fern
in my house.

I found it
under halogen
lights in a downtown
warehouse.

And now, three years
later, a lioness in
my care that I miss when
I'm away;

And a reminder
that love's
basic principle is
that love
will flourish
where we
place our
attention.

I go
outside and water
the Cacti.

I close
my eyes, face
the sun, put
both palms together,
and say:

"Greetings Day Creator. Greetings Lord Creator.
May love walk before us, behind us, and all around us."

And then I take four long breaths.

I used to breathe in the heat of the sun and breathe out fear,
visualizing the flames of that great expression of * burning away all fear.
But now it's best to breathe in all that fear and sorrow and breathe out some
nice non-fear and peacefulness out … sending it out out out there …

On the second breath I think of something Thich Nhat Hanh said,
something like
'Breathing in, I calm my body.
Breathing out, I bring peace into my body.'

Let me look up exactly what it is.

Ok I found it. It's:
"Breathing in, I calm my body.
Breathing out, I bring peace into my body."

On the third breath I just think and feel that I am breathing in God,
and breathing out God.

And on the fourth breath,

It's just breath,
in breath,
out breath,
nothing but the breath …

There's a Toilet Museum out there somewhere.

Hard to conceive of with our limited pee pee pea brains,
but it's gonna get us,
bring in some kind of age that is new.
Maybe the whole thing will turn out to be made of bee pollen.
And when it comes,
it will put one collective thought in all humanity's head:

"How am I this person?"

Birth
out heaven
in constellation gelatinous
splat.

Cloud.

Imp consciousness.

Your post-war spaghetti joy,
mashed potatoes and
Ruffles Chips,
              bright big pink ones!

Fun's funny
emerald eyes
burning and writhing and dying.

Shitty rainbow
Keep on truckin'

&
Check your nets.

You've made it
to the lost coast.
Get lost lost lost.

Now that you know

there is   no   home
there is only   home.

And the only

gift to give is

Thank you

for what is

&

Thank you

for what is

        to be.

> You are the only one
>   I try not
>   to love

and

>   you are the only one
>   I love.

There is no past.

Only remembering:

Love sucks out the poison, always leaves a little bit, buys ya a drink.

Love preys
on men
who do not
want to come
home
again.

I sometimes

rejoice

knowing

looking at the Moon

is free

and it's all I want

       Out of
       being

       A human
       being.

Instruction Poem 2

First
you make
your shapes.

Then
you paint
them in.

Dancing
with The Night Blooming Sardines

"Dear dying brother, die bright and don't look back."

Some people are no bullshit.

I am   some
                                    bullshit

I do   deeply love my life,
          enjoy my time,
my soul
blowing its nose on my body.

Finally, the warm cool
eve is not upon us.

Finally,

All there is
          is knowing

Now that you've died
maybe you won't die again.

I Like a Phone

When I see you sitting in the distance
in those black and white pictures,
I can fall in love with you
again and again,
every time.

And then
the phone saves the day:
a text, a picture of you up close,
and your greasy skin and stubby fingers
are what's really up.

Straw Leviathan
approaches
a blurred swarm
in the palms.

To a friend

Long gone,

I promise
to tell you

If you
overstay

Your welcome.

Wed Feb Fifteenth Six Forty Five pm ATM

I heard a little girl say,
"Hey Dad,
how 'bout we don't
go to the rave tonight?"

Can you believe it?
You see why I wrote it down.

Shit, I should've asked that little girl if she was ok, maybe called child
protection services ...
It didn't seem like she was really in any danger.

All those ravers
of my youth, curled
around speaker
cones, gnawing
on a pacifier,
are dads now.

Back to the poem:

Time to sing
an elegy for spring
& Soon one
        for summer.

Not Long After Earth

High desert.
No dream.

Reunion.

Moon of red meat & paper petals,
eyes old wolf arched
over cosmos.

God of 7-Eleven.

Reggae heroes.

In the poem,
I love you so much,
the moon is slowly moving away from the earth.
& There will be no eclipses in the future.

Magma Ocean,

Are the poems
just songs
with nowhere to go?

I miss you
so much.

No, I don't.

Shit,

I do.

At least the world
around me
is falling apart too.

Black egg jelly with spring onion,
glazed over
horse eyes
high desert
California.

With the runs,
on the rag,
on my dumbass
own now.

The Poem
is a human egg
walking into a pig's mouth
to get a good
              look.

San Francisco Poem

I am the ever-penetrating
fog, the embodiment
of egg-nog.

I am the shoreline
a-kneeling before
the Trans-adept.

I give myself
to the saddest of all
moms and join
her legion of clams
for midnight mass.

Obituary

Step Father and Step Mother
appear before you as two ossified banana peels,

With only seconds left
to undo a lifetime

Of earthly death.

You carry a torch,
a knife,
and rope.

You will never find us.

One white flower and a black she-dog,
the serpentine sea flowing out of you,
storm devouring you,

Til all is tranquility.

IHOP (Techno Quesadilla)

Time, the great molester,

Pisses some pipi,
then fly flies away …

Horseman, psychopomp,
and IHOP together
again, the great
ancestors, knowers

Of poetry's utility,
how we recognize
art outside
the museum:

Aging gongs.
Real demons.

The way back
begins to disappear,
& I too wish
I had Jessie's girl.

Somebody
out there
knows the way
you have felt
your whole life.

The cover band
in me goes
dumpster diving.

The doomed
man holds
an unplugged
microphone.

God …

The fish pie
was to   die
for,

only for
tonight, and then
also only
for the rest
of eternity.

I don't remember
anything
that happened
today.

My grip so loose,
that by nightfall
it all slips
away.

Spooky music spoken
to us:

Little   blue
ball,   little
blue   ball

I am much like you.

No need
for us
at all.

A chorus of horses among the dogs of Valhalla

It grew
like a festering
island,

The cold bells
of a wounded
we gotta go now.

Suicide after suicide.

I am proud of you, my cholo.

As my putrid
youth comes
to a close,
my gout-ridden
wife marries
your cuz.

The bomb shelter
has been bombed
&
we're off
to high heaven.

Guest

I long
to be

Remembering
this
later,

&

Not
writing it down
now.

What became of your new name

Mr. Baseball,

Let me look closely
at your serial number.

Let me look closely
and barely fail
to see.

I see that
sand is
a bit of baseball, but
weak-bellied.

I see the dummy dum dum of baseball carving deep recesses
into hot blue Patagonia
limestone.

I see
an Egyptian lady
dancing around her soup
knowing to first
polish a lion's tooth
with thirst
& all of Russia's spongy
weather.

Glory to those who
Baseball one another!

The best thing
about
some
          things
is that they don't
really
exist.

For my Father

Something   ends.
Something   begins.

All is worthy.

You are patience itself,

You who showed me
there's so much to learn
from the point

Of no return,
& that
the whole point

Is to leap
just as much
as the whole point

Of   the sun
is to be
     the sun.

You are simplicity itself,

Showing me
how to sing in my
no one showed me how to sing
way.

You are wisdom itself,

Telling me things
I didn't understand
like true
home is in each breath,

Until one day I did,
and now
that's how I'm not so lonely all the time.

Instrumental Music

Like an ex-con
at a nail salon

I'm hangin' on
like an ex-con

at a nail salon.
I'm hangin' on.

Rezo dirigido a la Madre

Copal
sagrado

A los ancestros
que han pasado.

Copal
sagrado

A los ancestros
que no han llegado.

I Suffer Too

Wake up
sufferer like me,
sufferer like me.

Gather up what power
power lets you gather.

When I am in the world
I am in love with the women
of abstract expressionism.

They dance in an overflowing manner,
make music in an ocean manner,
patient in the manner of the moon,
knowing God has no name.

Today is a day
of forgiveness.

I'm so pissed off at you.
I'm on my own.

        Pass through me, pass through me.

Leave me alone to plead to not be left alone.

Holy Man,
don't forget your bad vibes.

We arrive free
as beasts and become
something quite different
along the way.

Houston

As if to comfort me,
Fruit Cake On Aisle Ten
whispers, "nice
ears."

I'm touched.
It must know
I don't fancy
my ears.

It looked
beyond our sub-canine ways,
beyond all the glue in my esophagus,
beyond before Kathmandu was just green green green,
beyond the warrior and the corridor,

I mean, Condor …

Did you ever see that movie
Condorman?
I think about that movie
almost exactly

14 times a year … certain
scenes … mostly
involving Condorman's car.

M'lord, please
let me be
an extra
in your talkie.

Note Never Sent:
last night it rained
your last name.

Salt Shaker,
shake for me!

My Life,
like a wedding
ring
that someone keeps
losing.

"Put put put,"
goes the heart,

A little lamb
on a slab of stone.

Underwater sky

A pulse light

Underwater sky

"Put put put" …

Dead Dog Exhumed

Black bird

flew by,

helping

the way back

disappear.

Drawing Teeth

I drew
lots and lots
throughout my life.

Lines and lines of them.
Rows and rows of them.

And here,
in the remembering of all those drawn teeth,
I discovered a bed
of unused lungs,

All white
with blood,

All warm
with cancer.

Run into spine and bend neck incredibly.

These are
the dark ages.

The sun covered me
in motor oil.

& I
in turn
covered it
in Grade
B maple syrup.

My love has none
of its teeth
left.

Time is a quail,
not hungry,
but still lookin' …

Sierra Madres

Walking the trail,
I stop, smell
the juniper &
imagine reaching
around and plucking
two vertebra
from my back
& cracking
them open like a duck
egg and pouring
the yolk over
warm wet soil.

Remembering

The time
I went to prison
to visit
my father,

Him sitting in his cell,
writing a song,

Me saying please
don't add a key
change.

For the master
there is no
again.

Everything
that is   happening
                 happens
for the first

Time. Imagine
that.

I remember
you, but I don't know who
you are.

Geoduck,
look it up. Happy
Sunday to thee!
I'm going to temple soon,

But first Cacao
has flooded the streets
of Ho Chi Minh City
& the bells
of everlasting agony toll
toll toll and wishes
only graze us, never
coming true

And first,

The clouds.

She had come
all the way from Zimbabwe
to join
the Foo Fighters,
hoping for a fresh start.

But now,
so many years
after what
has become

So many years
after,

An old woman's
dying wish:

Get it over with.

Total   Pink Cosmos
in Square   White Cloud

Out of its mouth,
the blue light

Of no more
waiting.

Lines of
lightning standing still.

A thread of
red thunder
in your head.

A wrong done,
dreamed a way.

Apex bell,
echoing
endless
names.

In the house of
Leave This Body.

Instructions for a Dance

Paint eyebrows
on the sun.
Cover face
with red oil.
Do a funny thing.

Then say
this out loud:

My friend,

I've   stolen
the death-breath
from your mind,   stolen
the death-breath
from your mind.

When a beam shines through,
The inmate and the sun.

On Choosing a Name

On my knees
          wandering around
In the dream that all the soda was someone's braids
          wandering around
At the end tail of a bell
          wandering around
In the disintegrating thing
          wandering around
On the night you keep on dying
          wandering around
On the night you die and I think you've already come back as a little bug
that landed on my hand
          wandering around
In an expensive synthesizer that's been unplugged six months now
          wandering around
The house burnt down when you were a child, do you remember that?
          wandering around
In the sagebrush, with Mel
          wandering around
At the hospital, again
          wandering around
In I'll wait a few more days
          wandering around
What if we don't have a few more days?
          wandering around
Unimportant prayer now important prayer
          wandering around.
Choose a name,
Get unborn and be found
          wandering around.

In a man-made
deposit, a moth grew
over the walls
and told me
its name.

Now I keep it next to the
Dog Rose and Blue California
Lupine seeds.

Like koi fish in a state-funded temple,

I   gave all   I had
instead of what
                          I had
      to   give.

Like the rooted
masters (trees, get it?!)
and the blue mountains
of Heaven,

Why be   somewhere else
when   I'm here?

Only The Good Lord knows
what it all ain't about

Far
and further still

Into your holy molecules

Mother Teresa
just lost
her child
again.

Creamy Brick Transfiguration

Her nose,
like
the moon
asking,

You thinkin' what I'm thinkin'?

The Psychopomp Cracks a Cold One,

Re-writes an old song,

Rights a wrong, realigns
a star or two.

They said
you was a goner.

And they were right …

Non-linear fear,
you are
a formidable opponent.

I had yet
to discover how
frightened

You are
of being
seen.

Koan

Drowning
in urine but unable
to piss.

A tidy
cow tied
to a bridge.

Brains a-glistening,
the sparkling
flakes of friendship
lost.

On parole
you wrote
a song.

Back in
the pen
you wrote
a screenplay
called
The Purpose of Liquid
which ended
up turning into
a talk show
called
Tell Monk
about a monk

who gossips
with his audience.

Does the anthill have audience nature?

Does a star's heartbeat have wig salad?

Has anything reached
the horizon
via orchid realm?

Did the glittering
mouse cause
yesterday's luv
apocalypse?

Nope.

Onward.

Allow me to ask
again in a different
              way …

Heir jumps

to their death   …

dot dot dot

              …

And plants go whoosh!

Inside the flailing snake
as she strikes.

The body sinks.

All letters

Meet
when they meet.

Something something

Take a seat.

& From Tierra del Fuego
to the tippy top of Caracas …
little crab, search
my nipple

for the peep hole.

Motion, at best, is a slow caress.

Historic bridge: 1072, 1965, 1991.

Sizing up
the carcass
of a seed
I size up
a carcass seed.

Certain kind of song out   there …

Gather up a   little
          bit of it.

Mother   laughs

a great blue   laugh.

A dark blue   laugh

like those
clouds
up   there.

Bogotá

Winter is
upon us, even

Though it doesn't
get that cold
down here.

How kind The Good
Lord allows us
to sometimes not
see any more
than what's
necessary.

Stand on me.
Be patient with me.
God, I'm just a dumb ape,
hugging a dolled up
cucumber tree.

Ávila

I had no bottom teeth

and so

that's where you sat,

feet-a-danglin'.

Sun

Your name is
Tears of The Old Woman.

Levitating up there,

You noticed
that candle flame
looks like
a quivering
ice plant.

You are the best
at useless travel.

You are us,
waiting for Maitreya,
in the seed,
in the soil.

The police
in   the deeper earth
under
        the   earth
(that can be seen
if you look up.)

You are the one
who will help
me improve my

pregnancy.

You remind me
of Orson Welles
drunk
on youtube.

Just do anything?

Just do anything.

Yer right Bud!
I would indeed
like to be
        there.

But   for now
I am   here,
        where
I have
          always been.

Swallow the Sandstorm

Let
yourself

Begin

To mourn.

Reading Kabir at Your Funeral

TV taught me
that wearing an oversized sweater
signifies mourning.

It might have been Kabir
I read at your funeral,
only able
to almost just
cry. I
told your few drunk friends I
always thought of you as someone in one place.

And now you're
everywhere.

My few days in Houston
I felt death's particular cleanliness.

Sherrill gave me a blue vial of Your Ashes.

I've been living with it these past three years.
Now it's in a black suitcase.

Cologne headed for Turkey,
before transferring to New Delhi,
and then Benares.

Now checking into the corporate hotel,
far from the action,
none of the places along the Ganges available.

It's ok.

It's better this way.

More fitting

for what I've come here to do.

Gibberish cloud.

No need

for love

in your

eyes

when all's a brimmin' with it.

Grandmother

Standing by
the banks of the river
she built,

After three
days fasting:

An offering
　　　　to the stag,
an offering
　　　　to the deer,
and a hymn
　　　　to her hands.

Her hands.
Her hands.

And one
more time to bring
it all back
home:

Her hands.

Big Sky Cereal Magic

A small
Jewish cat
covered in butter

Merges
into Specific
Bald Man's
cave painting.

Tree of Life could be anywhere,
                              anything.

Elevator went

All the way up

To Specific
Black Man's
moon.

Last Words

Of course,
I forgot what I was looking for
while
                    looking for it.

1989

All of Aerosmith
kept a collective diary.

I read it.

It was awesome.

I remember, one page
said:

"Everything's starting to look like bagels."
—Mohamed

The Bird

Was
dead, but

The wind still

Filled its
wings.

Light

Is a manure pumpkin battalion.

In the creases of dawn, man
is ever at

War, half
an eye, an old
wooden
rope, sun

And moon, animal
fat and sprig.

And as fate would have it,
no Japanese elves
to put a little love
in your granola.

Close your eyes
and picture a giant blue nose,
one that looks like
Kenneth Patchen could have drawn it.

Close your eyes
and picture your biological father
pulling out all of his hair
until all that's left on top of his head
is a bright red
Pippi Longstocking wig.

Close your eyes
and see silver spheres
hovering between
your ears.

Close your eyes
& delicately remove
the rage from the grapes in your balding camera.

Close your eyes
& picture the terrible thing you are doing
and try to remember
that it's like forgetting the name
of someone that you know really, really well.

Close your eyes
& just for once
try not to rely on anything but
whatever it is you call God.

Close your eyes and exclaim
"those were some fine lookin'
locust guts!"

Close your eyes
as the crickets sing
their soft metallic song
& a wave in the air
goes missing for four lifetimes.

Well Well Well

Look what the cat dragged in.

If it isn't Hong Kong Charlie …

How the hell've you been?

Well, I've been good, you ol' son of a bitch.

Last Verses

The only thing
you know
            about
your child
            is that
you did not
want it.

            A crying
            shame made real
funny. We
            dance
scalpless,
            like children whose mouths are duct taped to exhaust pipes, swayin'
            like raisins.

The record you have just bought

Is of a horse galloping

Down wooden stairs
and more stairs
and more stairs
  and more stairs
   and more stairs
    and more stairs
     and more stairs
      and more stairs
       and more stairs
        and more stairs
         and more stairs
        and more stairs
       and more stairs
      and more stairs
     and more stairs
    and more stairs
   and more stairs
  and more stairs
and more stairs
and more stairs

One oughta be left alone
when one's out
looking for power.

You sit out there

For a good
amount of time.

Maybe something happens.

Maybe nothing.

Those are the rules.

Bob takes a picture of the light.

He's fascinated!

Clearly
in love
with the light.

Bob's in that light, and a bit like that light.

Bird says chhheeepp chhhoopp,

Mother
Teresa's Monastery
& leaves
on a leafless tree.

The light has got Bob
thinking
now about how
this must be why
mankind loves
gold.

I take a photo of Bob taking a photo of the light.

The light being a consort between realms,
Bob is rightfully in awe.

A walking woman in green pants pants ...
        then looks at a man with a red bag.

I have blood in my mouth, why?
Must be my gums, or I bit my tongue …

In the background
Someone blows their nose.

The light
goes from gold
to purple
to what religion is all about …

      Sun is setting.
      Sun has set.

I hatched,

as a child,

a plan

to invent

Windex.

I knew that Windex already existed,

and my plan was to wait until it no longer existed

and then I would "invent" it again

 & Reap the rewards.

I also thought about

adding rubber bands

and escalators to the mix

'Cause a good invention

is   a good invention.

Love Poem

The way you don't
                look at me
is   like
all the candles I hope
to someday   light.

End of Initiation

The child
bends over
to break
its neck.

I tell it,
"please,
pace yourself."

It stops
and lights a fire
and drinks it.

In a millipede
teeth manner.

Sundown God's Funnel Tongue

Exhaling moonlight,
some thing
that held warmth
             unfurls.

The towel, now
in flames,
with these little minotaurs,
and in their thumbs,
tiny leviathans,
and in their feet,
dirt filets,
and in their dirt filet filled feet,
crazy magic animals
on a red highway
covered in omelette sorcery.

Baby,
it's ok.

You can
admit
you moved

A mountain.

I finally found
the perfect
opportunity to start
reading the *Ribhu Gita*
that Dhayan gave me.

"Apparently Ramana Maharshi used to keep it next to him, even using it as a
pillow at times," said Dhayan, my actual first friend.

       Our moms were buds.
       We met as babies.

But when I opened the brand new copy,
a little flat bug crawled from the page and hid inside the spine of the book!

Shit!

So I left the book half-open,
standing,
hoping that
by this morning the bug would be gone.

Now
the book stands open,
no little bug in sight.

It's yet another version
of "The Sword of Damocles"

Except the lesson is not
to not care about the bug.

It's to leave the book alone

&

remember

a cookbook,

while useful,

has no food in it.

Ode

Oh Mr. Planters Peanut,
take me in your
arms.

Allow me a meander
on thine exquisitely
manicured garden.

Hats off! May you live
1000 years
and your heart never
harden,

Oh
Mr. Planters Peanut.

Like Numbers Fore
        Like Nur
Another, let's

be like that, ok?

ever Folding Over   Each Other

umbers Forever Folding Over   One

Prayer

What an instant
bond, to see them
kiss so quick
and their wives never
even knew.

It was as if
two strangers
at a strip club
at the foot of Mt Meru
had torn themselves free
from the fatty deposits
at the bottom
of a German zip-lock bag.

I know
what you're
thinking. But
too late.
I'm already
here,

Born into the forced
laughter that follows
forever losing
little bets.

Giri Pradakshina

Walking
the circuit

Remembering to

    "Keep your heart to the right of the object of devotion."

As I began,
a woman knew what I was up to

And sold
me a piece
of string to tie
around a tree,

But her vibes were no good.

Then a golden
dog began
walking by me, keeping
an eye,
guiding.

Toward the end
of the circumambulation, I bought
dog chews

to distribute to all the dogs.

A monkey appeared
and I gave it a chew
and immediately a colossal branch fell off a tree, landing within inches of
me.

"Do not feed the monkeys," it said.

I wished I had had a sack of carob

Though I've never seen carob sold that way and I'm not sure if monkeys eat
carob.

Now sitting,
removing
the little stones embedded
in my feet, wondering
if that monkey
wasn't Hanuman …

What do you think?

Listening to Alice,
in particular "Er Ra,"

A song
I hear and think,

"Oh, I've got to remember to ask Mel
to play this at my funeral."

Riding the subway
in Delhi,

How did those skinny
jeans that are somehow
also baggy make
their way here too?

I know
the most beautiful boredom,
a lighthearted,
nectar-like
boredom.

I know
an ambulance
whose baby has
just gone into labor,
blue locust guts displayed
for all
heaven to see.

I know
it's funny
we start doing drugs
because we want to be free
and we stop doing drugs
because we want to
be free.

I know
the beauty
of the moon
must be all
the world's Om.

Like Bombay Became Mumbai, Madras Became Chennai

From Feb 6-16, 1897, Swami stayed in the room that I am now sitting in.

Beautiful photo, lit eerily like '80s arcade.

Big, cold stones on the ground, soft and welcoming … so hot outside …

I sit.

Buck Owens' "Made in Japan"
and Prefab Sprout's "Life of Surprises"
keep weaving

in   and
out and
in   and
out, concise
like mosquitos.

Still the mind. Still the mind.

The music recedes.

It's distant and I'm closer now.

Keep sitting.

Sea sky dissolve …

Same thing
Sky sea dissolve

Same thing …

Piano music, like
one butthole,

Lerpin for the stars.
Austrian Astronaut,
moon canto.

My mini TV utterance thus spake:

I'm at that age where I might die soon,
but I've got to get this book of poems out.

Why is it that I have to?
Where does that need come from?

It doesn't feel like
it's because I think
they're so good …

&   This,
what I'm writing right now,
what is this?
Certainly not the poem
I pray not to die before
it's published.

I don't know why it seems so important, but it is.

I know it is, and deep down I also know it isn't, and then deeper down I
know it is, etc.
This is a kind of sanity, I think.

And I think you
understand.

I know you,
like me,
often feel

Like God's abandoned
lunatic, who
has to get
that book of poems out.

I want
the bull

To stick its
tongue
out
at
me
forever.

Kavijihvagravasini

Forsake me not,
Transistor radio from some faraway dream of a long long time ago.

That's fine.
Horrible sound,
you are fine.

In this terminal wing of the planet,
I arrive
to hear
of your
death again
and again.

And   sleep   for hours countless
before awakening
                       for hours
                                    counted.

Metallurgy

You shrink
into a gel,
a knotted door,
a lonely thing,
some coral.
You vote,
for a concise census
of world surveys.
You publish
a who's who
of emptiness,
combined with prayer,
& occasional thoughts
on cabbage.
You support
harmonium anti-family.
Now a different prayer,
I beg you to stomach pump
the world,
get a little Wisdom going.
Oh to know the difference
between your sex and a matchstick.
Celestial Beings dreaming on ultra-marine grasses
Google Translate Tantra
in a poem
made of water.
Are you a real live turtle?
If you do,
make a beeswax replica

of the Kaaba black stone
with Nagaimo bust
of African Melchizedek.
Insect sun,
Grand-Flower, near despair,
in some weeping realm, the sky was doubly emptied
&
a pug
is gravy
in your mouth.
Yes, for sure
it's pug-made
mouth gravy.

In conclusion,
trillions of little brains in your urine
& ritual scarification for all your compact disks.

Odd Bliss.

Holding a torch,
wait for me
underwater.

A man hangs
& gets
extra flowers.

Pearls

Creepy
doves cling to calm
pigeons flying
out of grandma.

Black ash claws.

Not Peruvian
cow nor goose,
but corpse
grease in her purse.

Now

Nothing,
but the sun
seeming to say:

I'm just as strong and beautiful right now
as I was on the day you were born.
Why aren't
you?

I love you

My religion is
the religion of dumbfoundment.
       Yakety yak
       Don't.

Make a fire
and let the flames burn away
anything
you might say.

That's our work, our job.

88

We didn't get it right
this round,
did we?

I'm afraid
        you're getting sicker.
I'm starting
        to think
        what I once thought
wasn't   such a good idea
isn't   such a good idea.

Broken water
made up of made up words,
        I blame myself,
        I blame you,
and   I blame everyone else too.

Knowing
the burden
will never be
lifted lifts
the burden.

In my Mahayana stroller,
off to see old friends …
In my fluid Jaguar mask,
off to see old friends …
In my high tech sneakers and HP Laser Jet printer/scanner ,
off to see old friends …

Moon

Gone, gone
                                away.

Mother,
                        the dream
of having
                        a dream
in which
you are explaining
                        the dream.

That's   the way

Mother
goes   away.

And with my poet's visionary eyes I can see things like a Starbucks brown
napkin blowing through the streets of Beijing all the way from very very up
close.

Blank and droopy
divorce court eyes
are but creamy grey
paper flower arrangements
tempting the life out of
a black hole's
unsettling insight.

If anyone says to you,
"no words can describe it,"
that's a good sign! Follow
that down to wherever it may lead ...

All senses   converge
til
one sense   is left.

Simply put, we gotta get free ...

But surrendering is hard work:
Check in & go through security, book
a hotel, see

A cow eating garbage

As serpents &

Piglets

Emerge from the dark, as you piss into a pool of scummy water.

After all,
it is wedding season.

& There are no
pictures of you
in this book.

And yes, the sun
does kill,
but it's the opposite
of murder.

And everything is torture
if you can't find the freedom
in knowing that everything
we do is   wet wet wet
and will someday be dry dry dry.

Black ink on dream garbage,
hand to phone,
sitting at the bus stop.

Long drive
night light.

Sattva
Rajas
Tamas

But now, I get ready
to go back to Japan.

I brush up
on the two main schools
and the masters' names
like tidying up my room
or a dip in a cold river.

I forget

most of what I read
but some sticks!

Boy oh boy,
you're a nice dry leaf
in the warm light
of winter.

Temple today
& caterpillar.

Obesity gene.
Synth weeps.

Rich worm castings.
A bro leaps.
An unimaginable expanse of brain.
A legendary phone call.

Gathering Days

Dehydrating your bloodshot ovaries,
while I run around in another man's body,
not filling objects
with myth.

Let's   go   beyond
what we have
            gone beyond

& Not let   how
            sad   we are
get in the way
of   how
            happy we are.

I'm so
sorry, My
Love, but
I can
only speak
in short
fragments
of sudden
expression.

That's the poem?

That's the poem.

Dance With Me, Muscle Mensz

Entertainment   helps you
                    forget.
Art   helps you
                    remember.

4am in Benares,

Sunrise and   cross the holiest river
to the sandy embankment
                    cross from all the ghats,

I sent your ashes off.

Asa just wanted to get back to you, Mother
and Gary couldn't take it anymore …

Only three years ago you took your own life.
I still think "maybe
                    you can take it back?"

But I am here, loving you both,

                    missing you both.

Your widows & I
wondering if that
hummingbird
that just showed up
is you.

First Day

I heard a voice
clear and loud:
I must remain chaste this trip
and not succumb to erotic impulses.

So I cut off the head of my penis.

This was good …

And after cutting my pipi off
I carried it around for a little bit,
and could even feel it expand and contract
now and then.

So I gave it to Will Lemon
and asked if he wouldn't mind
holding on to it for me
for the extent of the trip.

He agreed and put it in his pocket.

Will was very much one of Kali's consorts.

Now
I must go,
and be here.

I suggest
you do
the same.

Riding a Dead Horse

Hurry
home, hurry
home.

Maria

You are playing
such strange
chords.

I hear them hovering
over the canyon
like a homesick
hawk.

I see an empty ocean
under a blossom filled
bird.

I hear a brand new language
with very few
words.

I did not love everyone

So maybe
my life

Was a failure
after all.

Love Song

My love
is hiding
way up

There, top
of the tree.

My love
is hiding
way up

There, top

Of the air,

Even a little

Further up
than that.

I met the God of Flowers

I said

How do I know you're the God of Flowers,

can you prove it?

To which it replied:

No.

The Wind

Infinite Loneliness

All mine

All mine

Devendra Obi Banhart lives and works in California.

featherproof BOOKS

*Publishing strange and beautiful fiction and nonfiction
and post-, trans-, and inter-genre tragicomedy.*

Available at bookstores everywhere, and direct from Chicago, Illinois at

www.*featherproof*.com